coffee house poems

by
elliot m rubin

Copyright 2023
Library of Congress
ISBN 979-8-9922464-3-8 paperback
979-8-9922464-4-5 e-book
LCCN #2025902037

Published at
Monroe Twp. N.J.

Dedication
To my grandchildren
Shane, Isabelle, Jonathan, Carter,
Alexandra, Melanie, Mollie, and Madison

In memory of my father
Herman S. Rubin
who wrote poetry and prayers all his life

Preface

I believe poetry is to be read and understood by all, and it needs to be written, for the most part, in plain language for everyone's enjoyment.

Too often, poets write in-depth, penetrating poems where you need to be well-read and/or versed in literary minutia to appreciate the poetry, not this book or any of my writings. I try to write so everyone can enjoy a few moments of intellectual satisfaction without consulting a dictionary or encyclopedia all the time.

Disclaimer

This book of poetry is not intended to be read by prudes, political book-banning conservatives, and/or sexually inhibited and repressed small-minded dolts.

No human models were caught, used, or harmed in making the cover; it is AI-generated, at random.

What is Progressive Beat Poetry

Progressive beat poetry is a type of poetry that goes against the usual rules and traditions. It talks about social, political, and cultural issues to make people more aware and push for change. Here are some key points about progressive poetry:

- **Questioning the Norms**: Progressive beat poets often challenge and question the main social, political, and cultural ideas. They dive into complex topics like race, gender, and power.
- **Voices and Inclusion**: This poetry style aims to give a voice to those who are often ignored. It highlights stories and experiences that don't usually get attention.
- **Thinking and Talking**: Progressive beat poetry makes readers think about bigger societal issues and encourages meaningful conversations. It aims to start discussions and inspire actions towards social justice.
- **Breaking the Mold**: Progressive poets often play with form and structure, moving away from traditional styles to better express their messages.

Progressive beat poetry seeks to break free from traditional poetic conventions and push the boundaries of language, space-as-art, and expression.

Table of Contents

writing a love poem

it's not easy to write love poetry
first, you need to find someone
wine them
dine them
praise them
while you are on dates
make mental memos
later, write everything down
remember no rhyme, no crime
free verse can be terse
throw darts at broken hearts
write, write, write
forget couplets, tercets and sonnets
put your soul onto paper
a love poem is guaranteed
if not   chill with some weed

regrets

it is morning
fairy dust slips from her eyes
the mirror shows a fullness
a result of one drunk night
in the dance hall's restroom
    at the time
    with a maybe forever
though they only met
an hour before
he then became a never

now her swollen flower lips
will soon burp out an albatross
which she'll care for decades ahead
instead of a tropical vacation

fancy lace dresses and white shoes call
as she walks past windows of allure
in a well-worn winter wool coat
pushing a friend's loaned baby carriage
instead of sunbathing
on a hot caribbean beach
as lean, dark-tanned
glistening male bodies
drool over her
while she now wipes away
a baby's drool

killing time at the beach

i sit weary on a bench by the boardwalk in asbury park
retired, no work, no place to go in my old age
as the youthful lifeguard on his perch, and i, watch

elderly women
with walkers, health aides, oxygen tanks
walk step by tepid step as they pass

followed by heavy-set, middle-aged women
who wear tiny triangles of cloth
with bountiful bouncing breasts   who
ignore my wrinkled, weathered, crepe skin

their cellulite thighs and arms
ripple after ripple
like rows of waves crashing
crushing children's castles
as sand is flattened, and
submits to the sea

while young girls with flat abs,
postage stamp string bikinis
cover their taut, lean, tiny chests
sashay to attract male admirers
with the stamina i once possessed

along the shoreline, children scamper
as they scream with laughter
naked toddler bodies tanned by the sun
while mothers run after them
holding diapers in hand

i wish i could join them
unharnessed, carefree, a naked youth
to re-live   that time in my life

murder morning

it was   a muggy misty morning
doorbell rang   an hour before dawn
when the door opened   there stood
a bloody buxom beauty   about twenty
she yelled for help   her husband's dead
down the block   he's dead, he's dead
my body shook   filled with dread
called police   they found him there
slumped in a ball   with a bullet in head
no one knew   who did the dastardly deed
was it jealousy   or just human greed
his wallet's missing   ring and watch too
the wife thought   then told police a few
this day no one's caught   the culprits flew
everyone left   the street's silent again
it's now high noon   a morning insane
tired, i went back to bed   this day's too profane

raining pines

summer sun shines down
on the lone pine tree
hot rays streak through

long thin green needles
fall upon me
as i rest against the brown trunk
on top of dead tan pines
while a wisp of wind weaves itself
around me
cooling beads on my forehead
as it carries the scent
of the fallow farmer's field–
i remember well
when we walked at night
she held my hand
under the full moon
as the cows watched us kiss

a kiss so sweet

it lingers
in memory years later–
an unrepentant heartbreak
continues to ache
while i sit here
under a tall pine tree
one sweaty summer day

broken jar

early morning   the green tractor
sputters   roars to life then
heads to acres   of open fields
plows row
             after row   of fertile soil
to ready for seeding   the next spring day

stalks of wheat sprout   await a harvest
grains gathered   crushed
into fine wheat flour   bagged and shipped
to markets worldwide   then bought and
transferred to a small jar   for easier storage

with wet hands   grasped the container
then slips
       from five fingers
          to
             the
                floor
tiny shards of glass   mix with sifted flour
a farmer's weary work wasted

leaving

on a long walk
to the end of the station
i met many people
on my journey

some took any train
while many waited for theirs
others didn't stay
    they left the depot early
    ahead of their boarding time

now i'm at the platform's end

waiting

i remember
    those i've loved
    those i didn't, and
    the tears i shed

as my train approaches
    i hear it get closer
        it took longer than expected
            i'll have no regrets
when boarding

never always

forever
is not always forever
love is sweet and tasty
while it endures

teen angst is unbearable
they think it will last and last
until the thick oak tree
in the front yard falls, someday

dates in their twenties
are not dates, but adventures
exploring new people, personalities,
sometimes exposed, undressed

marriage and children
are expected for most
but some people
are not like everyone else

parents age and die
it's strange when adults
become orphans, now alone,
to face life without backup

forever is forever   sometimes

laughter

always saw the humor
in things others cried at
the guffaws silently kept inside,
most people are stiff
yet found those with ability
to laugh at his sense of humor
over dinner with friends
a quick wit found chuckles
the ability to float in a crowd
to turn serious frowns to smiles
his weapon of choice
he used it well with the nurses
as they came and went from his room
he threw out his last thought
a grasp for a last laugh

unlock

the old key looks good
    slightly worn and tarnished
right length
    ridges of teeth still line up
only when it slides in
    the lock won't open
no matter
    how many times it turns
the door stays closed
    until a newer key
bright and strong
    twists the tumblers correctly
and opens the passageway
    to her heart

star

i could-a-been a star
wanted to make music
youthful enthusiasm denied
career choice quashed
dad said not a good path;
at fourteen he obeyed
stifled creativity and delayed
though feet bound tight   growth stayed
not allowed to spread my wings
settled to hobby write for friends
felt what i might have attained
could-a-been   a star

last kiss

how do you say goodbye
to someone you love
moments before they die

motionless in bed
memories float about
kiss before they're dead

a lifetime of joy ends
illness suddenly occurs
pull the plug, depends

on doctor's final talk
before he turns to leave
my legs decline to walk

i stare and dare
death seems so slow now
time stops, a last deep breath

then the body coughs
a final rattle of death

to ron desantis

banned books
can be more powerful
than armies

with pen in hand   a
writer's enemies' quake
in their shoes, and
classrooms and libraries
with barren shelves
prevent reading   and thinking

written words are forceful
create revolutions
solve intractable issues
bring peace from war
write eulogies
for lost causes and dictators

morty the butterfly

the bright yellow flower calls to him
a siren's song only he can hear
always a loner, he flutters to it
focused sight ignores the obvious
long straight green fingers await
the petal's next beautiful meal

his cocoon buddy calls out
morty wait!
don't you see the danger   i do
let's visit the rose garden over there
he realizes she is more than pretty wings
they flew over to it   together forever

music

the midday southern sun   bakes the roads
while after sundown   the club's music's hot
guitars twang   drums beat rhythms
while electrified violins   cry as they play

two step circles   twirl 'round the floor
brown beer bottles   drip on the bar
the lead singer   steps to the mic
overlooks the crowd   and starts to sing

rhinestones twinkle   in bright stage lights
cowboy hats tilt   dancers move 'round
songs of sorrow soar   through the air
of lovers cheating   and families adrift

alone in the corner   she sits with her drink
tears stream down   from sad songs   so real
heartbreak tunes   bring back bad mem'ries
of children's deaths   and drunken beatings

today is today   tomorrow may not come
his lawyer spoke   of a broken-down love
she's depressed and filled   with regret
in early dawn's light   her music stops

on writing

poets don't write
in a vacuum
poems are
shaped by others
who influence
then lines are edited

written in stanzas
or free verse
when they start
to create works
their words
live in minds   forever

lisa gioconda[1]

a woman no one knows
with no known skill
is recognized by her smile
worldwide on sight

dead
five hundred years
researchers discovered
who she is, now
she gives hope
to struggling poets
who try for fame
to have their poems read
hopefully   before they're dead

---

[1] the wife of a Venetian merchant, Leonardo painted her – the Mona LIsa

on the way to the library

linda ronstadt sang
good to be in the u.s.a.
while i drove to a writing group, and
resisted flooring the pedal

the beat was intense and driven
as i passed parked police cars
on the sides of the roads
wishing i was on the parkway
to bury the needle past ninety
but twenty-five
is the required frustration speed
too bad, it's something i must heed

joey the black bear [2]

once there was a black bear
who's covered in white hair
he lived in the far northwest
captured and not given a test

they shipped him north to colder regions
couldn't thrive in the icy seasons
they thought he was a wild polar bear
discovered he had albino white hair

brought back to the lower forty-eight
then caught again with tasty bear bait
shipped him north like a piece of freight
another day they didn't want to wait

oh no!   park rangers said once more
he can't swim or walk on ice, oh dear
he's back   tagged by his ear
we'll ship him back, close the cage door

now joey the albino black bear
who could not live on ice or snow
was finally sent to live somewhere
in a sanctuary   where life is slow

---

[2] based on a true news story

eating

slaughterhouses
kill animals

they make porterhouses
to supply different meats
for human consumption
    supposedly
in a humane way

war
is a slaughterhouse
without porterhouse
to kill humans
not humanely
nor for consumption

boyhood dreams

as roustabouts
pull up stakes
the big tent top
drops on the center ring
animals secured
the circus ready
to pull out of town

leaves a small boy
in bed dreaming
of crazy clutzy clowns,
jugglers, tumblers and
lion tamers
wishes he could be one of them

until one day
maturity rolls along the tracks
becomes a lawyer,
makes a fortune,
remembers one evening
he wanted to be in the circus

buys a mansion in florida,
retires, goes deep sea fishing
lives his dream
in the circus of the sunshine state

back when

i liked being a kid
responsibilities limited
    take the trash out to the cans
    before dinner wash my hands
    a few times a day, walk the dog
    at night remember my prayers–
now as an adult with clout
more important things
to worry about

one night fright

cruisin' cross america
eight hours since a break
decide to stop for the night
when we see a motel road sign–
almost dusk,
we drive off route 80
into heavily wooded heartland
on tall, treed roads
until we see
a dim-lit sign ahead
for our intended rest–
a small, quaint place, not large,
about a dozen rooms, and
notice atop a nearby hill
a house, standing alone
against the moon's solemn glow
in extended silence
we check into
the *bates motel*

moon dreams

published in Lothlorien Poetry Journal 2023

moon circles   'round the earth
it watches   its birthplace
nightly   every rotation   no days missed
since sliced away   into space

a romantic moon   is my heart
alone   yearns to belong again
floats out there   with no way to return
since you cut me off   from your love

my newest son
published in Lothlorien Poetry Journal 2023

you're not my son
but you're flesh and blood
i was there for your arrival
raised you for eight years
our bonds grew strong
through mom's rights
and too many wrongs
my love never wavered;
more than a grandson
to me, you're my son

for twenty-one years
i've loved deeply
saw you off to college;
was there for crises or two
you are not my son
but to me
you are my son
forever

flowers

the sun shines brightly
on a cloudless blue sky
while in a house
built on love
locked in a basement
windowless
trapped, alone

don't bring me flowers
                    just the key
to unlock your heart

oxford

published in Lothlorien Poetry Journal 2023

he is unclear,
confused, and obtuse,
because he is not sure,
clear, or certain,
he wanted,
needed, or is required,
to use the oxford comma
when he writes a haiku,
sonnet, or limerick

one hour

i waited one hour   during a ceremony
before i was declared   married

two years later   my daughter was born
my wife was in labor   for only one hour

dozens of heavily armed police   waited in a hall
one hour in uvaldi   while 19 children shot to death

congress never earnestly debated   even one hour
for gun control   as they suckle on gun lobbyists' teats

to right-wing religious conservatives

this is not   your nation
               it never was
               or ever will be

america is   *our* nation
yours   and mine
forever   together

get used to sharing
               do your thing
               for yourselves
we'll do ours

don't help   the poor and ill
watch your voters   die off
we try to help   everyone

it's not about   small government
or not spending money   on aid
it's about caring   for humanity

everyone has a right   to their rights
even if it's against   your religion
but not theirs   deal with it

rainbows

are many colors
represent people
who are loud and proud
of their preferences in life

they convey
lifestyles of folks
in all variations
except those ultra-religious

who refuse to accept
everyone will be loved
no matter what sexual likes
desires colorless, bland rainbow

others

heartbreak and tears
they left home with fears
walked 1000 miles
to freedom and smiles

they thought

stopped at the border
kids jailed by his order
lost in the system
done with no wisdom

he broke mother's hearts
a policy enforced without smarts
a true crime against humanity
a heart filled with criminality

others drowned fleeing cuba
100 miles of boiling seas
the land of immigrants walled off
none allowed at the wharf

immigrants want in
we're all like them
we came from there
some though forget
from where and when

murder morning

it was   a muggy misty morning
frantic knocks   an hour before dawn
when the door opened   there stood
a bloody buxom beauty   about twenty
she yelled for help   *my husband's shot*
down the block   he's dead, he's dead
my body shook   filled with dread
called police   they found him there
slumped in a ball   with a bullet in head
no one knew   who did the dastardly deed
was it jealousy   or just human greed
his wallet's missing   ring and watch too
the wife thought   then told police a few
this day no one's caught   the culprits flew
everyone left   the street's silent again
it's now high noon   a morning insane
tired, i went back to bed   this day's too profane

self

being yourself is hard
society corsets your talent
it bristles and bubbles up
overflows onto humanity's floor
where it can no longer be ignored
or how you walk, talk, or think
truth matters
to yourself

courage

i don't need a bottle
for courage
to face a decision or situation
life's full
of uneven events

i'd think
what would john wayne do
he'd say *damn the torpedoes, full speed ahead*
regardless of facts
    sometimes
there's no other recourse

chaos appears
when least expected
i thrive on certainty
    not randomness
life often feels
like a las vegas casino
the world a giant roulette wheel
numbingly happenstance
        out of control
inhabited by strangers
who ignore me or
will service for a fee

yet i ignore both
then go about things by myself
in self-imposed bliss

naked in nature

i walk through naked woods
unclothed from mankind
neither paint nor saws
touch this virgin mountain forest
while small trout swim
where deer drink from
a meandering bubbling brook
as i wander alone

only god and i talk freely here
without censor or conflict
while turmoil
boils
in the valleys of the world
from where i came

taylor & 1975

it was pure love
maybe pure lust
what was to be forever
after 30 days a never ever

two people merged talents
ying and yang were in balance
worked together too well
people thought them quite swell

music is very creative
egos become primitive
they require a national tour
until one walks out the door

fruit lady's market

i like her
perfectly rounded grapefruits
desire her eggplant
the tiny ruby-red cherries
taste so sweet between my lips
it takes two hands to lift her watermelons
exhausted
satiated
i leave

nick's house across the street

a senior development has its pluses
there are also a few demerits
nick was 93 and fading fast
one morning i looked out my window

a black van parks in his driveway
two dark-suited men unload a stretcher
in a few minutes, they drive away
a filled body bag in the back

his daughters, one-week later
start to empty the house of small items
jewelry, family albums, boxes of papers
next week a green dumpster eats the rest

empty, the home is now a house
devoid of humanity and warmth
a for-sale sign is staked on the lawn
the biggest bidder buys the right   to die there

question answered

drugs and alcohol   will cloud the sun
happiness   is not a sleepy stupor
sadness reins   after tears run dry
when the exit door   slams shut
left in his mother   to be born alone
later father found   in filth-strewn room
rats climb over everything   to look for food
where does an addicted   baby go
when nobody is capable   of caring
while mother searches   for her next hit
social workers fret   baby's always wet

with a negligent mom   left unfed cries in bed
after methadone begins   put up for adoption

donald drumpf

i never knew
        an eagle could roar
often as a youth
        i read it would soar
it's valued higher
        than most carnivores
until one president's
        hit the floor

conspiracy, theft
        slept with a whore
thank goodness
        he was shown the door
stupidity smeared
        then spread into lore
state secrets stolen
        now secret no more

shown to guests
        and whoever would listen
alone with putin
        who knows what he said
don't know
        how many spies now dead
the people's powers
        went to his head

love laws

love is real
you can feel
yet not touch
nor see it

it reflects on faces

your heart can ache
even break
there is no medical cure
for a broken one

real love has high value
yet you can't buy it
there are laws
in certain states

marriage prohibited
between selected lovers
what they don't realize
is there's no such thing

as bad love

mom's moving

mom will be moving soon
though she passed years ago
i went through her treasures
previously, and placed them safely
in boxes, carefully wrapped in
bubble wrap for protection–
now i'm moving again, and she is coming
with me for another move–
she was not an astor or vanderbuilt
yet had a collection of jewelry
comprised of antique watches, rings,
and gold bracelets kept in an old, oiled
walnut box, hidden under her bed–
in her life, she hunted for these items
in small, manhattan, hole-in-the-wall shops
where she was on a first-name basis
with the owners; pawn shops in
atlantic city was another
favorite place to hunt, or haunt,
where high rollers needed quick cash
when she went on bus trips for gambling
but never played in the casinos
her money was spent in the stores of despair
picking over the bones of the desperate
to add to her collection

bedbugs

thrive under mattresses
behind headboards too
they're in almost all hotel rooms
to listen then munch on you

the stories they can tell:
    of honeymooner's first nights,
      to married lover's trysts,
        college drinking parties,
          after prom nights of embrace, and
           a president's porn star spanking

gossip papers would pay millions
to satiate the desires of their minions
those lousy blood-sucking pests
keep their tales close to their chests

they leave behind red-stained sheets
unbearable itchy skins
exterminators rush in
kill them for their sins

the day we met

the trains still ran
ocean waves tumbled
white clouds flew on blue skies
puppies wagged their tails
mom's lesbian lover left
dad's paramour became pregnant
sis announced her forthcoming divorce
my brother was engaged to a nonbinary person
you didn't answer when i asked you out

fifty years later, we're still married
my brother's husband died
sis remarried three times, now single
dad fathered more kids, different girls
mom moved on to another wife
the puppies were stolen and gone
we moved to where it rains too often
ocean currents brew devastating hurricanes
the trains stopped due to track disrepair

freight train thru dayton

one in the morning
fast asleep
in a rundown motel in tennessee
my bed shook, rattled, then i hear it
rumble rumble rumble
i open the door to see a long train
fifty feet away
across a dirt parking lot
iron rails not noticed at noon,
rumble rumble rumble
freight-car after freight-car
rolls forever
never-ends
a nation's strength on the move
the floor shakes under my feet
rumble rumble rumble
the train rides on
through valleys and pastures
of rustic america
slowly going somewhere
from rural nowhere
through forested mountains–
i close the door
go back to bed
before the caboose

divorce

she had an affair of the heart–
silent, it could never be spoken of
he was her husband's best friend
childhood buddies always paired

two couples who travel together
dinners out always a foursome
spouses trust each other
even if two were out, not present

one night she realizes her love faded
evaporated when they kiss goodnight
she imagines the one   not in their bed
wishes he is here   to kiss her head

wandering hands are imagined   not his,
thoughts of another as caressed all over
one day her dreams came true
life is no longer dreary and blue

she tastes the forbidden fruit
it is delicious–
years later,
it tastes like the one
put back in the basket

glitches

poetry is filled with glitches
some with real tongue twisters
read by longhaired hippy bitches
with flat chests and too-tight britches
in dark and dank city cellar bars
who fill old men's written memoirs
when they look back and think, what if,
as their eyes fill up and their noses sniff–
as young men, they listened too much
for hearts were broken with words that touch

zona norte, tijuana

they stand on the sidewalks
some wear tight short skirts
others in jeans or low-cut blouse
they smile, offer quick quips
bodies exposed to men to entice
one can see everything nice
best time guaranteed
prices cheap
only good time, try me
you can hardly walk past
they're teasingly fast
bars and brothels packed very tight
their neon signs shine bright at night
crooks and pimps are really tough
this area internationally rough
a higher death rate than urban detroit
girls of all ages pose to sexploit
it's time to go home to mom and sis
tijuana and tequila i will dearly miss

grounded

maybe it's an invisible glue
i never saw it, did you
nobody else ever did either
reasonable people neither
to stop and think

as we stand in america
how come the chinese,
on the other side
of a big round earth,
don't lose their berth
to fall off into space

way to go

always live in love
hate's such a burden
weakens your insides
decimates well being

give to others rebounds
in ways you might never foresee
when i care for people unknown
it always comes back to me

if you can, you should always give
money's a lot like water
flows fast like a sieve
it's not guaranteed permanent

marriage

jelly beans are different
their taste and color
dissimilar
or sometimes the same
yet two somehow stick together
and thrown in a bowl with others
as a wedded couple are in life

others surround them
politely taken one at a time
as they leave their society

until the bond
which bound
two beans together
brakes, splits apart,
a divorce of sorts,
a separation,
leaves one alone
to contemplate one's existence
and the meaning of together

contest audition

all-day, singers line up
a chance for stardom and cash
staff holds quick sings
to weed out the stinks

her husband's out of work
she performs at a local bar
around the corner, not far,
home late, fame her fate

spotlight shines, she sings a song
crowd goes wild, she cries like a child
years later, hit records too many
always on tour, her home's on the road

the money's big and bold
her voice is vegas gold
lured by pretty boys and lies
her marriage in tatters, it dies

i knew it was over

the door closed softly
her key turned slowly
to lock it for life-
she won the first contest
and the second one too
a teenage beauty winner
pictures in national mags
her narcissism reigned
the humility feigned
life went on without her
probably for the better
as my life focused on us, not i,
but rejection hurts, forever

july at the jersey shore

summer sun   torments
hot and humid   in the shade
skin burns bright   brittle
no relief   outdoors

ocean breeze   floats by boats
welcome light   cool whispers
the smell of salt   digs deep
in memories   forever burnished

sand heats up   burns feet
wet shoreline   feels relief
tides run out   pulls my soles
hard to balance   not to fall

almost eighty   my body aches
wild hormones   unrestrained,
many females   jump about
my youthful mind   runs amok

flower in my life

i hold her hand
    softly
my fingers touch rose petals
    delicately
her sweet smell swirls
    seductively
as it floats to my heart
    slowly

unseen

poets write about everything
love, life, death
yet readers never see it all

some poems are edited out
till there's nothing left to read,
their babies dead

marginalized

when men have power
they splay it

often finely focused
on women

influenced
by religious zealots

disregard inflicted pain
while half of voters

sit on their ballots
blind to political power

as they and their daughters
can suffer a debilitating lifestyle

that males never contend with

old myron schwartz and angel sanchez

born in poverty to a homeless mom
they were found wandering streets
by an elderly, lonely man
who took them in
fed them with meats and sweets
the seven-year-old boy
calls him father
years of love
never a bother, kindness
was the only house rule
old myron schwartz took him
to baseball games
played catch till dusk
bought him a bat, ball, and glove
often fished together by a stream

one day old myron schwartz stayed in bed
he could only move his head
the young boy wept and held his hand
and did not move, not one inch
 poppa i love you, please don't go
momma and i still need you so
the old man strains his arm
grips the boy's hand
    i give you my blessing, everything i own
    i love you.
then took his last breath
a life of empathy
remembered after death

want to love her

inside the bakery
i see a sweet cupcake
i'd love to hold in my hands
tenderly undress it
feel the cake's soft skin
against my fingers
press my lips on its sugary top
twirl my tongue on it
taste the moisture
savor the sweetness
imagine being alone with it
oh, how i want it for myself
yet i know it cannot happen
i already have a pastry at home
the next guy in line
wants this one too

builder of belts

many never met or knew me
yet hope i rot in hell
they heard i'm always grim
loud protests i'd always quell

i am king of the roads
used eminent domain
ran roughshod over toads
flattened them with disdain

built highways around new york
paved over poor in staten island
went deaf to those who'd squark
trucked in dirt, then fill a wetland

stole a boy's baseball dream
i wanted the dodgers in queens
instead, they moved, i always
want it my way   by any means

goodbye, brooklyn's only team
went three thousand miles away
tore the kids heart apart   by the seam
he never thought there'd be another day

newark 1985

the city's riots   are in the past
burned out streets   now a memory
of communities   no longer here
blackened timbers tilted tall   stand
as cemetery markers   of former homes–
bulldozed blocks   empty and bare   while
men walk around   with an empty stare
no work here   or anywhere
this city is dead   filled with dread

if you drive downtown to park   behind
bamberger's,   their lot is guarded
an empty city block   chain linked in
only feet away   from the building's back doors
you dash between   sloppy street whores

a crown jewel   of new jersey commerce
its floors are packed full   of better goods
this city's folks   cannot afford
no sales too low   to move them out
no shoppers   in a gleaming white's castle
just another cemetery marker
to tell of what once was   now in memories

near miss

my winning lottery ticket
    is only two numbers off–
a terrible accident happened
    minutes before i arrived–
the call i waited for hours
    finally came, seconds after i left–
a bus picked me up shortly
    before three people shot at the stop–
i almost married a narcissist
    a miss   i don't miss

young love

late night sins
the bottle spins
points to a girl
she smiles, he wins

leans to her
one kiss, a blur
so light and fast
quick love doesn't last

desires withheld
the love tree felled
uprooted, and dead
she played with his head

late night spins
nobody wins
nothing lasts, when
you play with sins

basement of war

their bodies strewn about on the floor
walls pockmarked with tiny bullet holes
a killing took place behind the broken door
men, women, children, all poor dead souls

this is not a traditional soldiers' war–
brutality and horror, war crimes galore
young girls still in diapers bleed out, before
their mother's eyes one dark deadly night

the new growth forests of two nations
cut down, decimated, their growth stopped
by hordes of bloodthirsty, emotionless pagans
generations denied, and a future evaporated

rose garden

years ago, i planted seeds
fed them, they rooted, and
grew tall with strong stems;
flowered to colorful blossoms

today i look at
a beautiful bouquet
gathered here
in love and harmony

my garden is bountiful

abortion

men have power
they splay it, focused

and influenced
by religious zealots

disregard pain they inflict
while half of voters

sit on their ballots
blind to their potential power

as they and their daughters
suffer a debilitating lifestyle

men never contend with

lovenotes

everything and nothing
we spoke for hours
words didn't matter
we were together

our hearts spoke in silence
to be with you
to see you
to be in your presence

love is funny that way
it need not be physical
your aura completes me
i need to be yours forever

red door

my legs are stuck
cannot step forward;
there in front of me
is her door,
only feet away

my shoes frozen
on a winter walkway
my courage iced
with cold weather,
warmth of conviction
evaporates
as i turn the corner

blood drains from my heart
the door splashed red
like a matador's cape–
a challenge of manhood
to meet her once more

apologies buried in my soul;
guilt flagellates my being

her face is in my mind's eye
i envy birds who fly south
while i, alone,
have to find the courage to say
i loved you once, but
was too young
to cherish
your bountiful bouquet,
forgive me

until the day i die

i don't want your kisses
or your tender caresses
this love has to end
you must stay a mrs

what we did was wrong
like an old country song
our passion is so strong
i'm tired, worn out, so long

go back to your main guy
this time it's real; goodbye–
i'll always remember you
until the day i die

revisions

writers constantly revise
similar to artists asking a muse
turn to the left a little
changing colors, deepening a hue
or painted over to make a change

poets must decide on tense,
use words to make sense
or delete a stanza or two
to convey thoughts
in metaphors

paint their pictures
in a reader's mind
sometimes in a form,
not easy to conform
to a set standard
or none, as in a
ginsberg beat poem
their words tend to roam

deep south in mississippi

magnolia is a beautiful tree
its trunk appears corseted thin
branches spread out, blooming
with sweet-smelling small flowers

tree roots are every-where here
white petals signify purity
contrast its ultra-conservative
traditional, racist politicians

though an attractive state
women can't make medical decisions
poor denied free federal medical care
votes gerrymandered are meaningless

carcass of the south smolders
embers of bigotry flare
keeps the state under the thumb
of ignorance and backward thoughts

dreams of death

my spirit's in free form
released from a worn body
unground
not earthbound
boundary free
i float about
able to see
through the fog of reality

heaven calls   yet
i never arrive
caught in a nether world
a different dimension
astrophysicists sought forever
left behind are bones and blood
freeing my soul to wander
my flesh unbound
feet off the ground
everything visible
i can't touch you
i want to touch you
i reach out to you
to no avail

my pain is gone

why do favorite things always end

fields of flowers bloom with spring
childhoods filled with memories
games played with youthful friends
and candy and cake birthdays too

adulthood brings its values
mature choices you have to make
petals fall to litter the floor, as
youthful exuberance goes out the door

nothing lasts, nothing remains
change is constant, enjoy your life
tomorrow will always come, but
there's no guarantee you'll be here

rights

there is a right and a left
often gun rights left dead kids
seems weapons of death have rights
dead people's lives are left with none
once the rights of gun death kill them

tiffany ann (aka tee)

slowly, cigarette smoke
drifts upward
finger taps the ash
into a half-filled water cup
while the television sits
on a shabby dresser, and
shows her narcissistic husband's perp walk
while she avoids the media, and
hides out in a south florida hotel

a mother's maiden named
credit card helps hide her,
untraceable, unnoticed–
she flees with a suitcase of cash
withdrawn from hubby's bank–
money he has to give back,
if he can, and
if they can find her,
before a fake identity buries her
in manhattan
amongst millions with millions
hidden away in plain sight

steak medium

the restaurant's beautifully dark
wood-stained sumptuous walls
brass chandeliers suspended
a classic old-style steakhouse

sizzling plates served by servers
filled to overflowing with steak
smashed potatoes buttered to death
a gut-busting carnivores festival

the farmer's field is sun-drenched
cows stroll slowly while munching grass
an artist's ideal pasture to paint
everything primal and surreal

yet forgets this while at dinner

dinosaur eggs

it's hard to find them today
they're so very rare
can't find them on a dare

hidden or crushed ages ago
yet some do exist
they're the principled ones

who put country over party
make laws to save lives
instead of cashing campaign coffers

from those who don't mind children
being blown apart in schools
or dying from poisoned air

spring issues

bugs are out
swat the biters quick
they are all about
    mosquitos get me sick

spring is definitely here
grab a corn stalk stick
those critters sit and stare
    squash them with a brick

cover up in the cold
dress down for summer heat
spring filled with mold
    as you dance to the beat

colors bright and soothing
ready for summer swatting

regrets

when you're not with me
darkness rules the world
my thoughts are for you

your phone rings
it goes to auto answer
you never call back

life would be better
if you were mine
how can i tell you

i've always loved you
because the sun won't shine
until you return

to start a life
bring my life
back to life

with you again
please
    i'm sober now

awake

eyes open first
coffee second
social media third
the day has begun

a pet mouse
runs on a wheel
gets nowhere
writers too, can relate

mondays come
week after week
month after month
weekends too short

a poet sits to write
a new life starts
in a world he creates
excitement begins

when poets   open their cage
they can go anywhere
dreams   can grow wings
then fly away

tennessee inbreds

please
    don't make fun of them
the republicans
cannot help be
backward thinking
gun loving racists
who expelled two black members
from their state assembly   but
kept a white one in office
when they demonstrated
against a lack of gun laws
after christian children were killed
in a christian elementary school
is this how christians care
that life is sacred

republicans offered
thoughts and prayers
at school kid's funerals
instead of doing something
to halt the sale of
weapons of death,
possibly
due to their ancestor's
appalachian inbreeding

gone

their faces
those young voices too
what they said
and where

my memory merges
many of them
in no order   though
it is crystal clear   like yesterday

childhood friends no longer
their lifecycle spent
their lives live on with me
cheating death   in memories

commonality

music differs
on where it's from–
country has a spirit
a twang you can hear
while soul has blues tones
mellow and soft

rock moves you
whether it's punk,
country or hard
your feet feel it

treble and bass
is a language
understood everywhere
no matter the region
no matter the politics
everyone understands it
everyone has it in them

bad day today

once a mountain of a man
ramrod straight
muscles on muscles
vice grip fingers of steel
he grasped my childhood fingers
gently, feather-light   as
we walked hand in hand

today his eyes are glazed over
with cataract cloudy blank stares;
he fills the hospital bed
from head to foot
covered with heated blankets
to try to warm ice-cold feet
his heart can't reach
while my nervous palm
rubs his purple-veined arm

i kiss his cheek goodbye   ,
one last time–
grandfather's work is done
he leaves me good memories
on a bad day

melting pot

how do you know
once the stew is mixed

no matter how you scoop
bits and pieces
of the ingredients
my country is mixed
different colors
different origins
different orientations

we are still one stew
indivisible
united
one people

worry and fret

i sit and stare
in front of the white, closed,
six-panel double doors
by my home office
while my grandson sleeps
contently on the other side
as i worry about his life

on the precipice of adulthood
there are cliffs awaiting
and valleys beyond deep
to welcome his possible fall

concerns
rampage through my mind
as he drives through life
about how to build guardrails
to protect him
after i turn off the highway
at my final destination

unattainable

there are many things in life
people strive to attain
to seek fame and fortune
others with empathy,
to help the unfortunate
try the improbable
think it is impossible
to know in their heart
it's attainable
but settle for less
than a gpa of 4.0

storms

whether
winter weather withers away
the strength of summer
turns skin into leather
in winter weather
snow falls like a feather
floats light
a weather sight
to remember
every time it is december
or even late november
you have to love
winter weather

repetition

he walks into her life
different bodies
same men
nothing changes
the way he treats her
submission built-in

doesn't feel empowered
not able to break the cycle
this is her life

until old age
he leaves her worn, weary,
undesirable to most,
    except
he always finds her again

cradle of liberty

a rainbow
comes after a storm
boston is as strong
as the cobblestones
in beacon hill
this city has a will
resilient and thrives
it bustles with hustle
in sports and commerce

america fed itself
on boston's fervor
a revolution started here
spread to form a nation
terrorists
picked the wrong city

senior dating

he had fish-sucking lips
octopus swinging arms
fingers which roam at will
money in his pocket
a flashy red sports car
seeks a passenger in the next seat

not a spiffy dresser
modest with basic flair
neutral tan is a favorite color
his choice of music
is fifties rock

his saving grace
to women of a certain age
who still desire to date a man
is not a car or cash that matter
or fashion-forward clothes
or even if he is married
but he *HAS* to drive at night

the pruner

by an open window
a wisp of inspiration
floats in
ephemeral in nature
heard in an inner ear
to guide the letters on a page
which was blank
only moments before

creativity's hard to explain
the proof it exists
are melodious poems
that skips on tongues
when read aloud

then a pruner edits the page
redlines lines, words, metaphors
until the poem
soars in reader's minds
or is crumpled and forgotten

forever

the morning after

her cheap perfume lingers
in my memory
purple feminine fingertips
slid on my skin
they scratched circles and lines
to spell
i l o v e y o u

last night
after the underground concert
we popped pills
she brought along
intimacy was spectacular,
as usual–
this morning
her blue eyeliner matched her lips

i turn over
to kiss my girl
but she isn't moving
                          or breathing,
her body feels cold to the touch
    clammy
don't know if it was the drugs
or the asphyxiation sex, i
miss my purple pill-popping girl

space

high in the sky
comets fly by
their tails of ice
betray their path
a destination
decided by chaos
they roar out
from the blackness of nothing,
unannounced
eventually crashing somewhere
nowhere known,
as the earthbound may never find out
similar to my lover, who left
in a trail of tears
and went somewhere unknown to me

devinity

i worship her daily
  the mother of life
nurturer who sustains
  the one to call
when distressed

embrace her
  feel love
wrong her
  feel wrath
proffer offerings
  she rejoices
holy and all-knowing
  god is a woman

dinner time

daylight is rest time
it's food scurries at night
when it thinks it's safest
but the feral cat knows

it knows to feed at dark
it hides in blackness
while cat eyes see all
claws sharp as teeth

P
  O
    U
      N
        C
          E
on dinner in the grass
a tussle with muscle
usually wins very fast

this time prey spins right
escape somewhat tight
leaps down below ground
dinner now out of sight

blue marble

look up at the white dots
you will feel minuscule
    the stars above your head
    in galaxies eons away
have observed
every footstep earth has taken
since the beginning of time:
    continental drifts
    volcanic eruptions
    great extinctions
    a renewal of life
    the burgeoning of unbounded knowledge
all in the twinkle of an eye

the greatness of man
is a false sense of image
    a mere dream
    in a continuum of time
to be unknown
in the far future
    when the earth
    crashes into the sun
and love ceases to exist

the end

for other books by the author

www.CreativeFiction.net

follow him on Instagram

elliot_m_rubin
people poems

www.ingramcontent.com/pod-product-compliance
Lightning Source LLC
Chambersburg PA
CBHW070759120626
46557CB00002B/672